THE BIBLE BOOK OF THE MONTH

THE BIBLE BOOK OF THE MONTH

JAMES E. DAVISON

BRIDGE RESOURCES
LOUISVILLE, KENTUCKY

Edited by David M. Dobson

Book interior and cover design by Kim Wohlenhaus

First edition

Published by Bridge Resources
Louisville, Kentucky

Web site address: http://www.bridgeresources.org

PRINTED IN THE UNITED STATES OF AMERICA
00 01 02 03 04 05 06 07 08 09 — 10 9 8 7 6 5 4 3 2 1

ISBN 1-57895-039-2

CONTENTS

INTRODUCTION

This book contains a reading schedule that will lead you through a portion of the Scriptures each day of the year. The readings will help to foster your spiritual growth either as you engage in private study and meditation or as you participate with others in a study and discussion group. Alternating between Old and New Testaments, the Scripture readings focus on one kind of biblical material each month—thus the name, *The Bible Book of the Month*. Usually the readings come from one book, such as Genesis or Matthew. Sometimes the readings come from several books, such as a selection of the epistles of Paul.

Each month, you will find a brief overview of what you will be reading. This will provide a guide for what to look for and what to concentrate on as you read the biblical material. By the end of each month, you should have a good sense for the book (or books) as a whole. It is hoped that you will also have gained a sense of the faith–life of the author or authors.

Take your time as you read each selection. Consider the words and the verses from different angles. For instance, look at them from the perspective of the writer. Picture how the audience would have responded as they heard or read the words for the first time. Ask yourself what those same words say to you now. Let the scriptural material soak into your soul.

To stimulate your mind and heart as you read, questions for reflection and discussion are included at the end of each overview. You can use the questions for your own private meditation and study. Read the chapter from the Bible first. Then, after you have looked at the question, go back to the chapter with that question in mind. Occasionally rewrite the question. You may even want to write some questions of your own. That exercise can help you to understand the verses more fully and deeply.

The questions for each month will also provide a valuable resource for group settings. If you are part of a group that will meet regularly, you can agree to study the appropriate questions prior to meeting. Then a discussion of the questions can be the center of the group gathering. There are enough discussion questions to provide at least two, and usually three, questions for each week of the year.

If you will be using this book in a group setting, you should know that the material can be employed in a wide range of ways: in small groups and in large ones; in groups where leadership is shared as well as where there is a primary leader or team of leaders; and in groups where the relative emphasis on Bible study, sharing, and prayer may vary greatly.

As you can see, *The Bible Book of the Month* can be used in a variety of ways. Whatever way you make use of it, I hope that it will encourage you to experience ever more richly that:

> The steadfast love of the LORD never ceases,
> > his mercies never come to an end;
> they are new every morning;
> > great is your faithfulness.
> > > —Lamentations 3:22–23

James E. Davison

JANUARY
THE BOOK OF GENESIS

January is a month of beginnings—the beginning of a new year and the beginning of "The Bible Book of the Month" program. Each month during the year we will read a different book of the Bible, alternating between the Old and New Testaments, so that at the end of the year we will have a better understanding of twelve important sections of biblical literature. These sections will provide an overview of the readings each month. They will offer some background information regarding important themes and messages to look for—and pitfalls to avoid.

This month we will read selected chapters of Genesis. Genesis tells us about the earliest beginnings of the created universe (ch. 1), about the earliest history of human beings (chs. 2—11), and about the first fathers ("patriarchs") of God's people, Israel. All of this is told not in scientific language, but in poetic, story language to get across basic truths about our existence: creation, fall, and the need for redemption.

Genesis is a fascinating book with wonderful stories that we have heard ever since childhood. It is also a rather curious book, with stories that were definitely never mentioned in Sunday school! It takes us to an ancient, almost alien culture. The presuppositions people had about life and death, friendship and marriage, religion and politics, are so completely different from our own that we may find the book difficult. Here are some things to keep in mind as you read through Genesis.

First, *people were polytheistic.* There was a general feeling that gods are more or less like humans: There are stronger and weaker ones, and there are nicer and nastier ones. In any case, there are many of them. Notice that God's appearances to the patriarchs—to Abraham, Isaac, and Jacob—are very much like introductions. Given that gods were so plentiful in Canaan, the Lord must describe the divine nature to people who do not know very much about the one true God of heaven and earth.

Remember this when you read about the command to sacrifice Isaac in chapter 22. For Abraham, a command from God to sacrifice his son would not have seemed nearly so shocking as it does to us. Perplexing, yes, because God had promised descendants through Isaac. But shocking? Not entirely, because some of the gods that people worshiped in the ancient Near East did demand child sacrifices. At this point, Abraham did not know enough about the nature of God to be sure that God would not really desire such a sacrifice.

Second, *the society was patriarchal.* The father was head of the family or clan. Continuing his line through his sons, particularly his firstborn son, was a father's highest priority. It is obvious that women in this society were considered to be property, and there was an underlying double standard regarding the level of moral behavior expected of men and women. That is why, in the pathetic story of Tamar in chapter 38, Tamar faced execution for her apparent adultery, whereas Judah was liable, at most, to censure.

Still, a certain friendship and caring does seem to have developed within some marital relationships. Reading between the lines, you can detect this kind of bond between Sarah and Abraham. It was more difficult for friendships to develop when the family was polygamous. When you read about Jacob and his two wives, Rachel and Leah, notice that there is a humorous note to the stories (chs. 29—30), but it is a humor that comes from trying to lighten the weight of what is otherwise a tragic, sad situation.

Third, *religious belief was very "this worldly."* Most people apparently did not believe in an afterlife. At death, all go equally to the tomb, or to Sheol, a kind of shadowy, unreal existence. You can see why the concept of living on through your descendants was so important. Look at God's promises (to Abram) in Genesis 12. None of them promises him directly what we would consider the core of our future hope—resurrection and an eternal life with the Lord. The covenant with Abram deals with "this-worldly" items: descendants, prestige, and a land of his own.

Genesis really does offer us "beginnings," doesn't it? Not just in the ways mentioned above regarding the origins of the world, humanity, and Israel, but also in the ways God began to reveal the divine nature to a sinful and fallen world in desperate need of help. In response to God's covenantal promises, we see the patriarchs take their first halting steps toward a deeper and fuller knowledge of the Lord. These beginnings show us how much more is needed—how great the distance is to the full revelation of God's desire that all people live together in harmony, peace, justice, and love. Even when this goal has been fully revealed, as in Paul's affirmation to the Galatians, "There is no longer Jew or Greek, there is no longer slave or free, there is no longer male and female; for all of you are one in Christ Jesus" (3:28), we see that God's people have great difficulty living up to the vision.

So it has been ever since. In a sense, all of us are just at the beginning, aren't we? The patriarchs, for all the differences between their culture and ours, are very much like us. They have faith, and they fall—just as we do. We can hope and trust, however, that just as God continually picked up these first believers and set them on their feet again, so God will do the same for us. That's the ultimate meaning of the covenant that we hear so much about in Genesis: It is a divine promise of constant faithfulness to God's people all the days of their—and our—lives.

QUESTIONS FOR REFLECTION AND DISCUSSION

GENESIS 1

Look at the structure of the six days of creation. Can you find a pattern here? What seems odd when you compare what is created on the first and fourth days? What can we learn about God from the way this creation account is structured in this chapter?

GENESIS 3

As you read verses 1–13, what do you see depicted there with regard to human nature and psychology? What do you think the real sin is in "original sin"? How might it impact us?

GENESIS 6—9

The twin themes of God's grace and God's judgment sometimes seem difficult to reconcile. Where do you find references to grace and judgment in these chapters about Noah and the great flood? How do they seem to be related to each other here, and what is your own perspective on the whole topic?

GENESIS 12

Imagine that you are Abram (Abraham). How would you have felt when God gave you the promises in verses 2–3? What are the promises, and what can you say about their later fulfillment in Israel's history?

GENESIS 16

What do you think of Sarai's treatment of Hagar? What of Hagar's response? How does God intervene in this situation, and what do we learn about God's nature?

GENESIS 17—18

So . . . why was Isaac given the name he received? What does it mean, anyway? (Compare Luke 1:37.) How might this name-giving be significant for the later life of Abraham and Sarah—and, indeed, for all the people of Israel afterward?

GENESIS 22

What is this terrible test of Abraham on Mount Moriah intended to demonstrate? Think about the elements in the picture: a father, a firstborn son, a sacrifice, a ram. How do these various elements tell us more about Abraham and God here, as well as point us toward the future?

GENESIS 24

Summarize this wonderful story in your own words. Why do you think Abraham decides to send his servant on this potentially dangerous journey? Which characters in the account are you particularly attracted to? Considering how Laban acts later, how would you describe him here?

GENESIS 27

Tensions have existed within Isaac's family for a long time (see 25:27–28). Those tensions now result in some unfortunate events. Describe the attitudes—and actions—of each of the four major players here (Isaac, Rebekah, Jacob, and Esau). Do you identify with any of them in particular?

GENESIS 29—30

The deceit that has already been part of Jacob's character seems to be a family trait! Summarize the events that occur in these chapters. How do deceit and envy bear bitter fruit for all concerned? Is lying ever worth it?

GENESIS 38

David, we know, comes from the tribe of Judah. Here we meet the original Judah himself. What do you think of his actions throughout this chapter? From your knowledge of David, can you see similarities in the characters of these two men? What do you make of the actions of Tamar? Do you think she was justified in doing what she did?

GENESIS 39—41

Verse 23 of chapter 39 tells us that "the Lord was with" Joseph. Given what we read in these chapters, there must have been times when Joseph wasn't so sure. Outline his various ups and downs along the way to becoming second in command in Egypt. What kind of person does Joseph seem to be (or become) through all of this? What can we learn from him?

GENESIS 50

Toward the end of this chapter, we see a tender exchange between Joseph and his brothers. Why are the brothers worried, and how does Joseph set them at ease? How might Joseph's comment to them help us understand God's response to evil, injustice, and pain in our world? Think of some instances in your own life when what Joseph says has been true for you.

FEBRUARY
THE GOSPEL OF MATTHEW

This month we are reading the book of Matthew. Because it is the first book in the New Testament, you might think that it was the first Gospel to be written. If so, you are in good company, because that is what people assumed for centuries. Only in the last hundred years have scholars, on the basis of exhaustive comparisons among the first three Gospels, come to general agreement that Mark was probably written first. It seems likely that both Matthew and Luke used Mark, along with other sources, in composing their Gospels.

Still, Matthew does hold pride of place among the Gospels. It is almost certainly the most often read and most beloved Gospel. It contains many of the riches we associate with Jesus Christ, beginning with the story of the wise men and the star and concluding with the Great Commission. In between, it offers us some provocative stories and parables of Jesus; the best-known description of Peter's great confession in chapter 16; and, perhaps most important of all, the Sermon on the Mount in chapters 5—7. Matthew is a wonderful Gospel, and it always makes for inspirational reading.

Matthew is often called a "Jewish-Christian" Gospel. It was written to address people within the context of the Jewish faith. Some of it would have seemed unintelligible to Matthew's contemporaries from a different culture, and you may find some things in it a bit strange too. For example, if you examine the genealogy of Jesus in chapter 1, you will discover that, although we read that Jesus' ancestry can be divided neatly into three sets of fourteen generations, the total number of names listed does not equal forty-two. Even more remarkable, comparison with 1 Chronicles 3 shows that Matthew has omitted three names. In a culture like ours, where accuracy and precision are so highly regarded, these features appear to indicate a certain sloppiness, if not incompetence.

You may have a similar reaction when Matthew quotes from the Old Testament to describe events in the life of Jesus. If you take the time to check the quotations in their original settings, you will discover that some of them do not seem to say anything very similar to what Matthew claims they prove. One of the quotations (2:23) cannot even be identified for certain with any specific passage in the Old Testament. None of this would have troubled a reader in Matthew's context, however, because Matthew used a style of interpretation that was common to the rabbis of his day. Not only was it familiar to his audience; it was also perfectly acceptable.

Unfortunately, acceptance of his methods of interpretation did not necessarily imply acceptance of Matthew's message as well. His primary point, and the main theme of the book, is that *Jesus is the Messiah. Messiah* means "anointed one," the term used for the kings of Israel. The whole of the book is intended to show that, in Jesus Christ, we have the fulfillment of all that the law and prophets had proclaimed (5:17). All of Abraham's descendants, therefore, ought to accept Jesus as their long-awaited king. The Jews as a nation ought to respond as some of them did briefly on

Palm Sunday, when they praised the Christ and sang, "Hosanna to the Son of David!" (21:9).

To understand what's going on behind the scenes, you need to remember that by the time Matthew wrote his Gospel the church was no longer simply a group within Judaism. It was becoming a distinct entity in its own right. Something like "Christianity" was emerging alongside Judaism. On the whole, the Jews had not accepted this new messianic movement, and some persecution was occurring occasionally against those who followed "the Nazorean" (2:23). You can detect the antagonism beneath the surface of the Gospel, and part of Matthew's goal is to encourage his readers to remain steadfast. It's as if he is saying, "Don't lose heart! What we're experiencing now—rejection by our compatriots— is what Jesus himself experienced from the scribes, priests, and Pharisees."

Another major theme in Matthew is *the need to live a righteous life*. Notice how often we read about the importance of keeping the commandments and doing "the will of my Father in heaven" (7:21). The Sermon on the Mount is full of elegant descriptions of how disciples of Jesus ought to live. Jesus also underlines the necessity of holy living in many of the parables. Look at chapter 13, where we have a series of "parables of the kingdom." The parable of the weeds is one example (vs. 24–30); the parable of the net is another (vs. 47–50).

Keep in mind that this intense emphasis on living a righteous life is not just a matter of doing the outwardly right things. The really central point, which Jesus makes time and time again, is that holiness must be from the heart (15:18–20). Ultimately, faith is based on an inner, or internal, relationship with God, rather than on external matters. This is why religious piety and practice are best kept out of public view (6:1–6); it is why family ties do not guarantee a relationship to God (12:46–50); and it is why the two greatest commandments are to love God and to love your neighbor (22:34–40).

When we do good deeds because of a heart that loves God (although none of us does this perfectly, of course), then we are what Matthew wants us to be—disciples of Jesus. In fact, the whole book is a kind of manual for discipleship. The twelve disciples provide a picture, both in their successes and in their failures, of what following Jesus means. Matthew's report of Jesus' many sermons is designed to help us live steady, focused lives following the Master. Thus, at the end of the book, observe Matthew's final hope for the whole world in Jesus' final commission to those who believed in him: "Go therefore and make disciples of all nations!" (28:19).

QUESTIONS FOR REFLECTION AND DISCUSSION

MATTHEW 1

The genealogy at the beginning of Matthew sets the theme for the entire book. Keep in mind that, for the Jews, the numbers 3, 7, and 14 (7 doubled) were holy numbers. Also, the consonants "DVD" in David's name total 14 according to the Jewish manner of counting. Now look at Matthew's summary in verse 17. What do you think he wants us to recognize about Jesus? Does this verse surprise you in light of the actual list of kings he gives us in the chapter? Finally, notice that some women are mentioned in the genealogy. Who are they, and what do you know about them?

MATTHEW 3

John the Baptist is a striking figure. How would you describe him physically, emotionally, and spiritually? What does he seem to be saying about the kind of people who should come to him for baptism, and what happens to them when they do? Reflect a little about what your baptism means to you.

MATTHEW 5

Notice the types of people whom Jesus calls "blessed" in the Beatitudes. Try to name some people in Christian history who exhibit the qualities stressed here. Have you ever known such a person yourself? Which of these qualities do you think you possess? Which might you like to work on?

MATTHEW 6

Roughly speaking, Matthew 6 talks about two dangers: (1) practicing religion for public show; and (2) being too concerned with worldly possessions. In what ways are Jesus' warnings here applicable to our congregational life—and to our personal lives? What can we do to ensure that we "strive first for the kingdom of God" (v. 33)?

MATTHEW 10

Jesus suggests that the life of a disciple will not always be easy. Look for some of the things Jesus says will happen to his disciples. Do you think that there are ways in which you suffer because of your faith? How do you feel about such sufferings?

MATTHEW 12—13

Here Matthew gives us some information about the family of Jesus. (John 7:5 adds some more.) Try to picture what life would have been like growing up with Jesus. Would you have believed in him? What does Jesus say about "family ties"? How might that affect how we look at others seated around us in our congregation?

MATTHEW 16

Look at Peter's "great confession" in verses 13–20. What does Peter realize about Jesus? How well does he understand what he is saying? What does it mean for us today to say that Jesus is the "Messiah"? In what ways should that knowledge influence your life?

MATTHEW 18

In verses 23–35, we read Jesus' parable of an unforgiving servant. What is the point that Jesus is making, and how does that relate to our own attitudes and actions? Compare the words in the Lord's Prayer ("forgive us our debts, as we also have forgiven our debtors"—Matt. 6:12). How does this parable help to illumine the relation between our forgiveness of others and God's forgiveness of us? What do you think it means to "forgive your sister or brother from the heart" (v. 35)? Why is that sometimes hard for us?

MATTHEW 19—21

In the Sermon on the Mount, when Jesus says, "Be perfect, therefore, as your heavenly Father is perfect" (5:48), he is indicating that we need to take the Christian life of discipleship very seriously. What dangers, though, can be associated with the attempt to be, if not absolutely perfect, then certainly very good? How might parables like those of the rich young man" (19:16–30), the laborers in the vineyard (20:1–16), or the "two sons" (21:28–33) help clarify how we ought to live, as well as how we ought to view others?

MATTHEW 24

Not unlike today, people at the time of Jesus were interested in— and sometimes eager for!—the "end of the world" to come. In this chapter Jesus fields a variety of questions about the end. What kind of principles does Jesus suggest regarding our attitudes to the end times? How do they comfort, and perhaps challenge, you as you live in this world?

MATTHEW 26

Try to "feel" your way into the story of Gethsemane (vs. 36–46). Imagine that you are one of the disciples. What do you think you would be experiencing knowing all the threats against Jesus, as well as his own strange mood on this dark evening? Why do you think the disciples can't remain awake with Jesus? What about Jesus himself? What would he be feeling in this situation?

MATTHEW 27

Picture the awful scene at the crucifixion in verses 37–44. As Jesus is mocked and reviled, can you see how this could be "the last temptation of Christ"? Compare the temptations in the wilderness by Satan earlier in Matthew (4:3–11). In light of verses 45–46, does Jesus' situation seem any different from the first temptations? What would the consequences have been had Jesus succumbed to this temptation?

MARCH

THE BOOK OF EXODUS

This month we return to the Old Testament as we read much of the book of Exodus. At the end of Genesis we left the family of Jacob in Egypt, with an aged Joseph predicting that God would arrange to bring the family back to the land promised to Abraham. Exodus tells us how this came about, but it tells us much more than that! It also tells us how this extended family became a nation, the people of God called "Israel." In the Exodus, God redeems the people by leading them out of Egypt, taking them through the wilderness, and eventually (although this takes us beyond the book of Exodus itself) establishing them as an independent nation in the Promised Land. That God had done this in the past is the reason that Israel later trusts in the Lord (sometimes in difficult circumstances) to again redeem them from affliction and trouble. This is why you will find many references to Exodus in later Old Testament books. If you want to see some examples, take a quick look at Psalm 114 and Zech. 10:6–12.

In and around the exciting, often awe-inspiring events recorded in Exodus, we learn some tremendous things about the relationship of God and this people. Here are two of them.

First, *God alone is sovereign*. Remember what we saw in Genesis—a general polytheistic assumption that there are many gods busily influencing this world in which we live. A companion assumption is that the gods are connected to a certain geographical area, and their power extends only to the borders of their territory. Imagine how insecure this could make you feel if you had to travel to a foreign country!

One of the fundamental emphases in Exodus is that such limitations do not apply to the Creator of heaven and earth. The very name that God makes known to Moses, "I AM WHO I AM" (3:14), is a clear indication that God is absolute and eternal. When we read about Moses and Aaron facing the Pharaoh and his court magicians (chs. 5—12), we are watching a kind of contest between the God of Israel and the Egyptian gods. Each of the plagues involves an attack on something that held sacred meaning for Egyptian religion. The implication to be drawn from these plagues, therefore, is that the Lord stands above all other so-called gods and religions.

Second, *deliverance comes from God*. This seems like a rather obvious point to us, but it seems to be one that the Israelites (and not just them) had trouble remembering. Enslaved to the Egyptians, the children of Israel have no chance of effecting their own release. But the Lord steps in on their side, and, against what appear to be hopeless odds, God leads Israel out of bondage. Even the Red Sea cannot stand in God's way.

Notice that what we are uncovering here in Exodus is the primary biblical idea of the covenant. Already with Abraham (and with Noah, for that matter), we have seen the Lord initiate a new relationship of trust and friendship. The term *covenant* is used because God enters into a kind of contractual arrangement that contains both promises and obligations. For Israel, the obligations are to live in the world as an obedient people of God. All of the laws in the second half of Exodus and in later books are given toward that end. The climax is the Ten Commandments, which serve as a kind of summary and symbol for the whole of the moral law.

Unfortunately, the children of Israel don't hold up their end of the bargain very well. Repeatedly, they fail and they fall. This is why the tabernacle, with its strange rituals for sacrifice and atonement, is so important. As you read, concentrate on discerning how the tabernacle is the embodiment of a promise both that God will be present with believers and that the Lord God remains present even in the midst of human failure and guilt. This is important not only for Israel, but also for us in our own walk with our God.

The New Testament develops this same covenantal theme when it talks about "grace" (Eph. 2:8). By grace God redeems people from slavery to sin and death (1 Cor. 15:56–57). The ultimate means that God uses, of course, is Jesus Christ. We are moving through Lent and will soon arrive at Holy Week. Along the way you will see many reminiscences of Exodus if you are looking for them. As you meditate on the meaning of the Last Supper, Good Friday, and the miracle of Easter, let your mind wander back to the Exodus. Marvel at the steady commitment of a God who is willing to do so much to redeem people from sin, injustice, and death—both then and now.

QUESTIONS FOR REFLECTION AND DISCUSSION

EXODUS 2

What kind of person does Moses appear to be? As the great deliverer who frees Israel from the Egyptians, he already does two things in this chapter that foreshadow the spectacular events of Exodus. Can you find them? Notice the question in verse 14. In light of later events, what deeper meaning might be contained in this question? See John 11:50–52 for a similar symbolic statement.

EXODUS 3

What do you think of Moses' excuses when God speaks to him

through the burning bush? Reflect on God's name, "I AM WHO I
AM." What do you think it means, and how might it help to sustain
or encourage your own faith?

EXODUS 7—10

The plagues involve a kind of assault on the "gods" of the
Egyptians, and through them the divine sovereignty and power that
belongs to the true God are manifested. What basic cycle of events
occurs in connection with each of the plagues? Why do you think
this goes on ten times instead of five, or two, . . . or just one? What
kind of connection might there be between this cycle and natural
tendencies that may be a part of all of us human beings?

EXODUS 10

Verse 27 uses a phrase, "The Lord hardened Pharaoh's heart," that
we have read a number of times in the last few chapters. What do
you make of this strange phrase? Does this mean that Pharaoh can
be absolved of guilt in the mistreatment of the Hebrews? What is a
"hard heart" anyway? (Compare Ezek. 36:24–27.)

EXODUS 12

What are the basic elements in the Passover celebration? Think
about the elements and what they seem to symbolize. Reflect on the
further meaning of some of these elements (for example, the blood)
in light of the sacrifice of Christ on Calvary. In ancient Israel, the
death of the firstborn symbolized the death of the family as a
whole. Why would this be the case? How does this understanding
throw further light on the final plague—both for the Egyptians and
for the Israelites? How can it also help to throw light on the cross
of Christ?

EXODUS 15

Look at Moses' "song" after the deliverance at the Red Sea. Pick
out some of the claims he makes about the God of Israel. Can you
name some times when you have experienced some of these things,
to one degree or another, in your own life? How did you respond,
and what has been the lasting impact on you?

EXODUS 19

God makes a covenant with Israel, and Israel agrees to do all that the Lord commands (v. 8). Although later the nation doesn't keep its end of the agreement very effectively, it appears that God has high hopes for the people here. What do you think the implications are of God's statement that Israel is to be "a priestly kingdom" and "a holy nation" (v. 6)? What meaning might this have for the church (and our church)?

EXODUS 20

How many of the Ten Commandments can you name (in whatever order)? Notice that the first four deal with our relation to God, whereas the final six pertain to our relation to other people. Do you think this order is important? Can you really love God and not love your neighbor? What about vice versa? Compare Jesus' answer in Matt. 22:35–40 about the greatest commandment in the Law.

EXODUS 21—23

In these chapters we encounter some of the first "legal" material that attempts to provide justice and order for the Israelites in a rather difficult environment. Look at the kind of rules that are set forth. Can you find any themes here relating to such things as treatment of other people and property, voluntary/involuntary actions, treatment of foreigners, killing human beings, and so forth? Where do you see justice and grace in these rules?

EXODUS 28

Look at the costume that is designed for the high priest here. Among the details, notice especially some of the primary colors that are mentioned. You might consult a Bible dictionary to find out what those colors symbolize. Notice the ways in which the twelve tribes of Israel are associated with the priestly garb. How do you think the people would feel about this?

EXODUS 32

The people have just seen many great marvels performed by their God. Can you imagine why they would now so readily decide to

worship a golden calf? Does the Lord's statement (vs. 9–10) that
God will wipe them out and start over with Moses seem just to you?
Would you have replied to God as Moses did? What further insight
does this give us about Moses' character?

Exodus 33

What do you make of the statements that God spoke to Moses "face
to face" (v. 11) and that Moses was allowed to see God's "back"
(v. 23)? How might we reconcile this with our usual assumption
that God is purely spiritual (see John 4:24)? How do you normally picture God?

APRIL

THE ACTS OF THE APOSTLES

In some ways Acts is the most exciting book in the whole Bible. It is not the most fundamental book, because that honor must go to the Gospels. The Gospels tell us about the life of Jesus, which is the climax of God's action in bringing salvation to a fallen and needy world. Without Jesus Christ, we would have nothing. Still, Acts is tremendously stirring. It tells us what has happened because we do have Christ. It is a fascinating story.

Acts begins with the postresurrection period when Jesus appears to the disciples, preparing them for their mission to the world. As yet, they are not really close to understanding God's intentions, for they ask whether the Lord is now going to "restore the kingdom to Israel" (1:6). It will require a good deal of work before they can truly recognize the implications of Jesus' response about (1) receiving power through the Spirit (2) in order to witness not only in Jerusalem and Judea, but also in Samaria and throughout the world (1:8).

Use these two points as a kind of guide as you work your way through Acts. First, *the disciples are to receive the power of the Holy Spirit.* Chapter 2 takes us right to the heart of the matter. At Pentecost, the disciples receive the very Spirit of God, and this makes all the difference for the rest of the story. From hesitant and half-convinced followers of Jesus, they become courageous, confident apostles. Peter preaches a bold sermon (2:14–36) that persuades many people, and he employs the power he has received to heal a lame man at the gate of the temple (3:1–10).

Luke, the author of the book of Acts, relates how amazing signs and wonders continue to be performed by the apostles (5:12), causing many people to listen to and accept their message that Jesus is the Christ, the Messiah. For instance, the apostles are released from prisons (5:19; 12:3–11); Philip is directed to the Ethiopian (8:26–40); and Paul is converted on his way to Damascus (9:3–6).

These amazing signs and wonders are one side of what the New Testament tells us about the Spirit. The other side is more inward: The Spirit dwells in believers. God is no longer simply external to us, but the Lord also lives within our hearts. Paul and John, especially, underscore this aspect of the giving of the Spirit (see Romans 8; John 14—16). Acts tells us more about the outward and visible manifestations of God's Spirit. Both sides are highly important, of course.

Look for references to the Holy Spirit as you read through Acts. If you wonder why we don't seem to see such marvels in our day, it may help to recall that Acts refers to a mission, or outreach, situation. Stories of events like these are more common on the mission field. Apparently, while the Lord will employ dramatic means to establish the church, God prefers less sensational methods once the gospel has become familiar to a culture.

For us, this implies that God depends on our willingness to proclaim Christ and to live faithful Christian lives to get the gospel message to others. We, too, are promised the presence and power of the Spirit, but it tends to come in a more quiet, more inward fashion. Naturally, the danger here is that we won't detect the presence of God's Spirit. As you look at the Spirit in Acts, also look for the same Spirit in your own life.

Second, *the apostles are to be witnesses throughout the world.* The story line in Acts begins in Jerusalem, but it expands ever outward, ending finally with Paul in Rome. Along the way, the disciples learn that God really means to bring others, even Samaritans and Gentiles, into the church. If you remember our own problems at all levels of society—racial tensions, distrust of foreign cultures, animosity because of political or religious views, and cliques in schools—you will understand how hard it must have been for these Jewish disciples to step out into a wider society and to affirm that God really, truly loves all people equally with the Jews.

Again, Pentecost sets the stage. The tongues understood by people from many different nations hark back to the Tower of Babel (Genesis 11), where the sinful intentions of humanity resulted in disunity and separation. Now, by the Spirit, God begins to work in the opposite direction, enabling people to understand one another and thereby bringing them back into one group, the church.

Note that it is the Spirit that makes this possible. The familiar refrain "We are one in the Spirit; we are one in the Lord" summarizes this perfectly. Unity of Christians, one with another, is a watchword in Acts. In chapter 15, which records a kind of council at Jerusalem, the apostles and elders affirm that God really, truly loves the Gentiles equally with the Jews.

Not everyone agrees with this decision. Paul is plagued consistently by "Judaizers," people who insist that Gentiles must first convert to Judaism if they want to follow Christ. But their cause is doomed, and universalism is victorious over nationalism as the main line of the Christian church expands into the whole world.

I hope that, as you read Acts, you will be refreshed by the vigor of the earliest Christians. May what God did through them in the first century help us keep in mind what the Lord can do through us in the twentieth century as well!

QUESTIONS FOR REFLECTION AND DISCUSSION

ACTS 1

In verses 1–11, Jesus describes the new situation that has come about because of his work of redemption. The disciples only partially understand him, and they seem to want to hold on to the past. Can you find the same tendency in yourself? What are some of the reasons we human beings have this inclination, and how might we deal with it?

ACTS 3

Put yourself in the place of the man who had been lame from birth. Recall that lameness was seen as a deformity that meant ritual separation and distance from holy things (see Lev. 21:16–24 regarding the priesthood). Experience the event at the beginning of chapter 3 through his eyes. How would you have felt if you were him? When you take into account Isa. 35:5–6, what does it mean that the lame man was "leaping" in the temple?

ACTS 6

Is it hard for you to believe that the early disciples were quarreling this soon? What created the dispute, and how did the apostles solve it? Are you aware of such disputes in your congregation or denomination, or in Christendom as a whole? How might the approach here be of help?

ACTS 9

In this chapter we have the famous story of Paul's conversion. Describe what happens to him. What kind of changes do you think take place in him through this event? At the same time, Paul is called to be used for God's purposes. What is his call, and—from your knowledge of his later life—how is it fulfilled as time goes on?

ACTS 10

Peter's vision makes up one of the main turning points in the Acts of the Apostles. Why does God (have to) give Peter this vision, and what is the content of it? Why do you think it is so hard for people—including people in the church—to put aside prejudice and racist attitudes? What can we do about that in our church and in our society?

ACTS 12

Throughout this chapter, we read about "Herod the king." This man is a grandson of the famous Herod the Great. You may want to read about the complex relations and intrigues in this family in a Bible dictionary. What kind of person does this Herod seem to be? How would you evaluate the personal and political motives underlying his actions?

ACTS 14

At Lystra (vs. 8–18) we get a glance at the kind of religious beliefs held by people in Asia Minor (modern-day Turkey). What do they seem to believe, and how do they apply their beliefs when Paul and Barnabas come to them? Describe the message Paul tries to get across to them. Why do you think it was so hard for those people (and for us?) to understand this message?

ACTS 15

The meeting in Jerusalem recorded here has been called the "first church council." It is a shame that it has not served more often as a model for handling disputed issues in a peaceful and upbuilding way! What is the issue that must be resolved? Who are the main speakers, and what resolution do they come to? What do you think of the outcome?

ACTS 16

Verses 6–10 show us how Paul's missionary activity took him from Asia Minor westward into Europe (Greece). Luke is particularly concerned to stress the action of the Holy Spirit in the growth of the early church. What does he say about the Spirit here, and how does Paul learn about God's message for him? Have you ever had such a dramatic experience of the Spirit? How do you usually experience the Spirit in your own life?

ACTS 20

Paul's visit with the elders from Ephesus in verses 17–38 is often used to help describe to new officers in local congregations what kind of leadership responsibilities they are accepting. What is Paul's basic advice to these leaders? In light of verses like verse 32, how do you think he felt about entrusting the leadership to them? Have you ever had to turn over something (like a project or a position) to someone else? How did you feel about it?

ACTS 21

James and the elders try to forestall the danger Paul will face if he returns to Jerusalem (vs. 17–26). What are they worried about, and what strategy do they develop to safeguard him? As you continue reading in Acts, you will notice that the tactic doesn't work. What does this tell you about Jewish and Gentile feelings toward each other at the time? How can we break down these kinds of prejudices and hatreds in our own age and circumstances?

ACTS 23

The first part of this chapter shows how Paul can disrupt proceedings in a courtroom when everyone appears to be united against him. How does he divide his antagonists? In what ways would they be in agreement against Paul? In what ways would they disagree?

ACTS 26

In his defense before King Agrippa, Paul says with some astonishment: "Why is it thought incredible by any of you that God raises the dead?" (v. 8). Are you as astonished about that as Paul seems to be? Why do people seem to think the resurrection is incredible? How do you picture the resurrection?

MAY
THE FIRST BOOK OF SAMUEL

The book of 1 Samuel may be one of the most intriguing books in the Old Testament. It is an adventure story with exciting tales of men and women, love and hatred, friendship and rivalry. Interspersed with these motifs are the usual accounts of armies and warfare. In short, 1 Samuel has all of the ingredients to keep our interest and attention.

At the same time, some things in this book will strike you as alien—possibly even incomprehensible. Israel is a traditional agrarian, clan culture, and it is vastly different from the environment in which we live. The story of Elkanah's two rival wives and their troubles in chapter 1 illustrates this. As you make your way through the book, you will run into other cases of what seem to us to be strange patterns of life.

Still, there is something very familiar about 1 Samuel. That is probably because the book concentrates on three people who are very much like us: Samuel, Saul, and David. A fourth person,

Jonathan, is also sketched in some detail. By the end of the book, we have a rather complete picture of their characters—for good and for ill. As you observe their personalities and interrelations with one another, here are two central points to bear in mind. They will help you keep track of what is going on as the story unfolds.

First, *the primary theme is the establishment of the kingdom of Israel.* Samuel, the last of the judges, is the link between an earlier, rather anarchic time, and a period of greater governmental stability. Samuel anoints first Saul, and then David, to be king of Israel. The purpose is to give "the anointed one" the blessing of God's Spirit for this special task. It is worth noting that the term *anointed one* is "messiah." Thus, when we call Jesus "the Messiah" or "the Christ," we are referring to the fact that Jesus is God's final king. This Jesus is the ultimate ruler who will reign eternally in the kingdom of God.

This is why it is so important to trace Jesus' human genealogy to David (Matt. 1:1; Luke 1:32; Rom. 1:3). It connects Jesus to the prototypical ruler in God's earthly kingdom. Israel always looks back to David as the first true "messiah." In a sense, then, 1 Samuel tells the story of David's rise to the kingship. This makes the story of Saul's downfall all the more tragic. Saul could have been the prototype of the "messiah." If he had remained steadfast in his faith, today we might call Jesus "the son of Saul." That is a good reminder of how serious the consequences of our choices in life can be.

Second, *the Philistines are ever present in the background.* The Philistines were a warlike people who emphasized physical prowess and technological supremacy. Facing them, the Israelites were always at a disadvantage. Philistine culture accentuated military capability, and Philistine religion, with its warrior gods, was a cult to the aggressive, violent tendencies in humanity, particularly in males. The giant, Goliath, is the logical extension of Philistine faith; he symbolizes trust in the ability of human strength to vanquish any opposition.

The battle between David and Goliath is a visual portrait of the constant conflict in Israel to abandon the faith of Israel (reliance on Almighty God) in favor of the faith of the Philistines (confidence in human ability). Saul himself struggles with this choice. Imperceptibly, but inexorably, he begins to rely on his own capabilities, and the results are predictable. In the end, he becomes paralyzed when he finds himself faced with a superior hunk of humanity. David, in contrast, keeps his eyes focused on the Lord God and emerges victorious.

Isn't this same danger still present today—in our nation and in ourselves? Isn't it true that whenever we begin to rely on human ability or physical prowess, whenever we evaluate people—especially the elderly or the handicapped—primarily in terms of production, and whenever we take refuge in our technological superiority, we move very close to the camp of the Philistines? At such times perhaps it would be wise to glance in a mirror to see whether the image that gazes back at us is that of David . . . or Saul.

QUESTIONS FOR REFLECTION AND DISCUSSION

1 SAMUEL 1

Picture the situation in Elkanah's household. How is it similar to the circumstances in the household of Jacob and his two wives, Rachel and Leah, in Genesis 30? If you were Hannah, how would you have reacted? Does her response to the disappointment in her life have anything to say to us?

1 SAMUEL 2

Reflect on "Hannah's song" (vs. 1–10). Look for references to some main themes in this song, such as God's majesty, trust in God, and the need for humility. Notice how Hannah's language indicates God's reversal of the circumstances of life. Can you recall some similar words of Jesus in the Gospels? Have you had any experiences like this in your own life?

1 SAMUEL 5

This chapter provides an interesting account of what we could call a clash between the God of Israel, Yahweh, and the god of the Philistines, Dagon. If you look at the story as a kind of satire on Philistine religion, what does it tell us about which god has more power? How does the story do this in a humorous manner?

1 SAMUEL 7

In light of what you have seen of Samuel up to now, how do you picture this man? his faith life? his family life? If you remember anything of the time of the judges, how does this situation seem to be similar to those days? (Remember that Samuel is considered to be the last of the judges.) How might he serve as a role model for you?

1 SAMUEL 8

This chapter tells us about Israel's desire for a king. There seem to be a number of different motives at work here. Do the reasons the people offer for wanting a king seem sensible to you? Put yourself in Samuel's position—as someone who is nearing the end of his life and has served God faithfully. What do you think of Samuel's reaction? How would you have reacted to God's response?

1 SAMUEL 9—11

Usually, we think of Saul in terms of his failures as king. At this point, however, concentrate instead on the beginning of the story of his kingship. What kind of characteristics does Saul exhibit? What is praiseworthy about his actions and attitudes? It is often said that Saul had everything going for him. What kind of things give that impression? What might lead someone like this to go wrong?

1 SAMUEL 14

Jonathan is a relative unknown among the Old Testament heroes of faith. This episode, however, speaks volumes about his courage, faith, and wisdom. Contrast the image of Jonathan in verses 1–30 with that of Saul at this stage in Saul's career as king. How much truth is there in the old adage, "Like father, like son"?

1 SAMUEL 15

"To obey is better than sacrifice" (v. 22) is an important principle in the Old Testament. It can also be found in the books of the prophets, as well as in the teaching of Jesus in the Gospels. What does this principle have to say to us today?

1 SAMUEL 16

Recall how Saul was chosen to be king (chs. 9 and 10). Here, in verses 1–13, we see Saul's successor being anointed by Samuel. How do the events surrounding Saul's and David's selections seem similar, or perhaps dissimilar? Why do you think David was chosen?

1 SAMUEL 20

This rather long account of David and Jonathan's relationship tells us a good deal about true friendship. What do you find here? Compare verses like Matt. 5:9; Matt. 10:34–39; and Rom. 5:7–8. How do the actions of David and Jonathan illustrate the points made in these passages?

1 SAMUEL 24

This chapter, and chapter 26 as well, tells of an opportunity David has to eliminate Saul. If you had been in David's shoes, would you have reacted as he does? Why or why not? What does this story say about the advice in the everyday proverb "The Lord helps those who help themselves"?

1 SAMUEL 25

This long chapter relates an incident in David's life where David doesn't look particularly heroic. Nabal certainly doesn't either. The real hero is Abigail. What are we told about her, and what can we learn from her character and actions? (What do you think of her reward—being added to David's growing harem?!)

1 SAMUEL 27

What do you think of David here? What about his faith and courage? his wisdom? his honesty? Does this seem much like the person who is a "man after God's own heart" (13:14), much less the one who fearlessly faces the giant Goliath? Can you remember times in your own life when you have been similar to David in any of these ways?

1 SAMUEL 28

The "witch of Endor" is a strange story. Long ago, we are told, Saul had banished mediums from the land. What leads him to seek one out at this point in his life? Look at Deut. 18:9–15. What is wrong with mediums anyway (or astrology and other "black arts")? What might this say about horoscopes in the daily paper?

1 SAMUEL 31

This distressing chapter tells the final act in the story of the king that Israel wanted so desperately. There's a reminder of Israel's high hopes for Saul in the anecdote about the men from Jabesh-gilead. Look back at chapter 11 to see why they take the risk they do. What is your reaction to the course of Saul's life? Do you know of parallels to this story in the lives of others you have heard about? What can we learn from this for ourselves and for our church?

JUNE
THE BOOK OF PSALMS

For centuries the Psalms have offered inspiration and encouragement to people. The book is composed of collections of psalms written during many different periods of Israel's history. If you remember the picture of a young David playing the lyre at Saul's court, you will have a feeling for how deeply rooted in Judaism the psalms are. In honor of his significant role in the development of the psalms, David came to be known as the psalmist par excellence of Israel.

Sometime after the return of the Jews from the Babylonian exile, a final collection of psalms was made, and the book became a focal point for worship services not only in the Temple but also in other settings in Jewish life. You can find a clear glimpse of this in the Gospels. Just before leaving the Upper Room for the Garden of Gethsemane, Jesus and the disciples "sang a hymn" (Matt. 26:30), a reference to one of the psalms that was normally used at the close of the Passover service.

The psalms are still central to our worship today—more central than you may think, in fact. Just recall the psalms (like Ps. 23) or the portions of psalms that many of us memorized as children. Or think of the language in our Sunday morning liturgy in calls to worship, prayers of confession, and responsive readings from the Old Testament. Or look in the indexes in our hymnbook to find the hymns that are based on the psalms. It is surprising how many there are!

This month we will be reading a selection of psalms. They are incredibly varied: from hymns of praise, to cries for help, to confessions of sin, to songs about Jerusalem and the Temple. The most important thing to remember about the psalms, however, is that they give us an inside look at intimate, open, and honest conversations with God. We see people of faith praising and glorifying God's name, but we also see them expressing doubt and hesitation, confessing uncertainty and fear, and praying for understanding and assistance.

That is how the psalms can help us. By showing us how other human beings have communicated with the Lord, the psalmists offer us a model for our own relationship with God. Here are three things to watch for as you read the psalms this month.

First, *the psalmists praise God with abandon.* Listen to some of their exclamations of praise: "The heavens are telling the glory of God" (19:1); "Make a joyful noise to the LORD, all the earth" (100:1); "Bless the LORD, O my soul, and all that is within me, bless his holy name" (103:1). These writers see God revealed in all of the wonders of the universe. They foster a humble spirit in themselves as they recognize that the almighty, sovereign Lord of heaven and earth rules over everything.

Second, *the psalmists are brutally honest.* People are often puzzled by the calls for retaliation and vengeance against enemies and evildoers in the psalms. The middle section of Psalm 69 is a good example. When you read this kind of passage, it may help to remember that this is not a theological statement about how God deals with evil people, but rather a record of how people felt as they suffered injustice and what they said about it to God. We may be uncomfortable with what they felt, but their remarkable honesty in relating their feelings can serve as a reminder of our own less-than-perfect thoughts and desires, and it can arouse in us a stronger sense of our need for a compassionate and merciful attitude toward others.

Third, *the psalmists hold onto faith regardless of circumstances.* Psalms 37, 42, and 73 are good examples of this. So is Psalm 46, which was the inspiration behind Martin Luther's great hymn "A Mighty Fortress Is Our God." These psalms can help us in times when troubles come, even when waves of misfortune seem to crash over us relentlessly so that we feel as though we are hanging on only by a slender thread.

There is something in the psalms for everyone in every situation. Don't just read them; ponder them and meditate on them. Let the rich experience of God contained in the psalms saturate your soul and focus your heart on the one and only God. May reading the psalms this month compel us to confess ever more fully, "As a deer longs for flowing streams, so my soul longs for you, O God" (42:1).

QUESTIONS FOR REFLECTION AND DISCUSSION

PSALM 1

This psalm sets out in stark contrast two "ways" that people can conduct their lives. How would our lives look if we followed each of these alternative ways? Which do you find more appealing, and why?

PSALM 14

An *atheist* is defined as a person who does not believe in God. Does the person referred to in this psalm necessarily fit that definition? What is it about this kind of person that so upsets the psalmist? How might the feelings expressed here be applicable to our own twenty-first century world?

PSALM 19

God is portrayed here as the Creator and the Giver of the Law (Torah). How might the psalmist see creation and the Law as similar? What value does the Law seem to have for people? Is there a place for law in the context of the gospel and faith in Christ?

PSALM 22

You can see quickly why this psalm is called a "lament." How do the words describe the psalmist's situation and feelings? Do you know of other people who have held onto faith while undergoing such deep suffering? How do you think you would react in similar circumstances?

PSALM 27

Notice the combination of assurance and anxiety in this psalm. What statements of faith do you find in the psalm? What kinds of things seem to be creating fear and misgivings for the psalmist? Can you affirm the psalmist's final words, "Wait for the LORD"? Why or why not?

PSALM 33

This psalm sings a wonderful melody of praise to the Lord God. What sorts of things does the psalmist affirm about God? What is the purpose of praise, or adoration, and how do you see it manifested in services of worship? Reflect on what place it has in your own prayer life.

PSALM 42

The psalmist seems "down" while composing this psalm. Look for the longings and fears that surface here. How does the psalmist deal with distress, and what part does faith seem to play in this? In your own words, try writing about the feelings and hopes expressed here.

PSALM 46

This psalm is the basis for Martin Luther's familiar hymn "A Mighty Fortress Is Our God." Look at a copy of the hymn to find how Luther drew from the psalm. Notice the tumult at the beginning,

and the quiet at the end, of the psalm. How might that be sugges-
tive for our attitude to the events of life?

PSALM 69

In this long psalm, the author appears to be in dire straits, with
dangerous enemies close at hand. Notice the contrast between "I"
and "they" as the psalmist depicts his situation. Parts of this psalm
return in the Gospels as we read about the sufferings of Jesus
Christ. In what ways are the attitudes of the psalmist and of Jesus
similar or dissimilar?

PSALM 84

Recall the structure and the significance of the Temple in ancient
Israel as you read this psalm. Imagine the feelings of pilgrims as
they made their way to Jerusalem, singing a psalm like this. Do you
ever find similar feelings welling up in you as you come to worship?
If so, when and why?

PSALM 91

Security in difficult circumstances is a keynote in this psalm of
trust. Notice the various descriptions of dangers faced and protection
provided. In light of the temptation of Jesus in the wilderness (see
Matt. 4:6), notice too how words of the Scriptures can be misused.
Think about how assurances like those in this psalm can properly
be used in an often uncertain world.

PSALM 116

Gratitude is the central theme of this marvelous psalm. From the
sense of despair in the face of a life-threatening situation, to the
thrill of release when the danger is past, the psalmist depicts
thoughts and emotions in a gripping way. What sorts of reactions
does the psalm call up in you?

PSALM 130

There is a plaintive cry to God for support and aid in this psalm. The
words *hope* and *wait* appear in a number of places. What do you think
they mean? Do you find it easy or hard in your own life to "wait" and
"hope"? Are you waiting or hoping for something right now?

JULY
LETTERS OF THE APOSTLE PAUL

After a month of reading the psalms, you are likely to find this month's material to be quite a change of pace. The four letters we will read were written to a number of different churches, and they combine intensely personal comments about Paul himself with very deep theological themes. Mixed in and through each letter is a relentless stress on the necessity of living a good, moral life.

We often think of Paul as the teacher of salvation by faith, not by works. It may be surprising, then, to note Paul's constant accent on ethical admonitions and moral exhortation. If so, remember what "justification by faith" really means: It affirms that we do not (we cannot!) live a good life in hopes of deserving God's salvation. Rather, we receive salvation solely as a gift. We are intended, there-fore, to seek to live a life pleasing to the Lord out of thankfulness to God for the salvation we have already received.

When you stop to think about it, isn't this a truth that Western society urgently needs to rediscover? With so much emphasis on achieving success and acquiring material goods—as well as on eating, exercising, and dressing correctly so that everything about us appears to be in optimal condition—aren't we tempted to think that our value depends on what we do, what we accomplish, and what we achieve?

Paul's point, however, is that nothing we do is sufficient to make God smile on us. As long as we are trying to make ourselves worthy, or good, or valuable, the focus remains on *ourselves*, rather than on *God*. What is needed is a change of attitude—a recognition that, "warts and all," we have value and we are acceptable to God. As you read these letters, notice that this theme of "justification by grace through faith" is discussed in depth on a number of occasions (Romans 3—4; Galatians 2—3; Ephesians 2). There are any number of other themes to look for as you read. Here I want to suggest two to watch for especially.

First, Paul repeatedly emphasizes *thankfulness*. This, for Paul, is the reasonable response to God's justification in Christ. At the beginning of his letters, Paul almost always comments on his thankfulness for a variety of things in the lives of his readers. The primary exception to this is the letter to the Galatians. Given the problems he was having with that congregation, it is not surprising that Paul was not feeling particularly thankful when he wrote to them.

A comment in Ephesians sums up the kind of attitude Paul took in his own life: "giving thanks to God the Father at all times and for everything in the name of our Lord Jesus Christ" (5:20). He recommends the same attitude to us in a well-known verse that is worth memorizing: "Do not worry about anything, but in everything by prayer and supplication *with thanksgiving* let your requests be made known to God" (Phil. 4:6; italics added).

Second, look for the spirit of *joy* that saturates Paul's life. This is the major theme of Philippians. If you underline each place where the words *joy* or *rejoice* appear in this epistle, you will get a good feeling for how fully joy permeates Paul's soul. What makes this even more remarkable is the fact that he wrote these words in prison, while facing an uncertain future. Another indication of how important joy is for Paul is that it appears in his list of Christian virtues, which he calls the "fruit of the Spirit" in Gal. 5:22. Paul must have been an incredibly joyous person—one who drank deeply from the well of life and enjoyed every moment to the fullest.

The "fruit of the Spirit" brings us back to where we started: the constant, and sometimes disturbing, stress on the need to live a serious Christian life. Why? Not to earn salvation. Not to achieve value and goodness. But rather to please God, to show our thanksgiving for what we have received, and to express our joy to the One who has not only created us but also provided us with redemption. As Paul would put it, "Praise be to God for the great gift of Jesus Christ, our Lord!"

QUESTIONS FOR REFLECTION AND DISCUSSION

ROMANS 1

In the first seventeen verses of this chapter, Paul introduces himself to Christians in a city that he has not yet visited. What do you learn about Paul as you read his comments? What does he have to say about Jesus Christ and the gospel?

ROMANS 4

Abraham is of great importance to Jews. How does he now play a role for Gentiles, too, according to Paul? Notice how he guards against the idea that the Law is essential for salvation. How does circumcision fit into all of this? What are the values (and dangers) in external religious rites or signs?

ROMANS 6

Notice the connection between union with Jesus Christ and baptism. How does Paul link the baptismal act to Christ's death, burial, and resurrection? What implications for our lives does he draw from this link?

ROMANS 9—11

Paul is very much concerned about how his own people, Israel, fit into God's continuing plan of salvation. What kind of conclusions does he draw as he works through this complex issue in these—also complex—chapters?

ROMANS 14

Think about Paul's comments about judging one another. How might we apply these thoughts to our own setting—in church, in our families, and in our community?

ROMANS 16

Reflect on the final doxology at the end of this letter. Can you find traces of major themes that Paul has discussed earlier? Compare these words to the opening salutation. Why is this an appropriate way to conclude this letter?

GALATIANS 1—2

In other letters, Paul can take his apostolic authority for granted. Here he has to reassert that authority. How does he justify his right to speak as an apostle? What is the connection of his apostleship to the gospel message he would like to preserve? How does Paul's rebuke of Peter at Antioch fit into all of this?

GALATIANS 4

Paul speaks of an adoptive relationship that God established with those who believe in "the fullness of time" (v. 4). Why is this relationship important, according to Paul, and how is it distinguished from a legal relationship? What does it mean to you to be a "child of God"?

GALATIANS 6

To a troubled church, what are Paul's final admonitions? What would the Galatian congregation look like if the members followed the advice in verses 1–10? How would your congregation look? Are there any specific items here that you could apply in your own life immediately?

EPHESIANS 2

The Gentiles, Paul suggests, were once far away from God. How have they been brought near, and what kind of relationship ought to exist now among all members of the church? In the life of churches around the world today, where do you see continuing dividing walls, and where do you see examples of Christians living like the "household of God" (v. 19)?

EPHESIANS 5

What is it about the relation of Christ and the church that makes this relation an apt image for a marriage? Consider ways that love and respect can be fostered in marriage.

PHILIPPIANS 1

Paul indicates that there may be a variety of motivations for proclaiming the gospel. What is his response when others preach from what appear to be questionable motives? What kinds of motives for preaching have you seen? What is so important about motivations anyway?

PHILIPPIANS 4

In the first nine verses of this chapter, what kinds of behavior does Paul urge his readers to practice? Concentrate on a few of the exhortations here. Why are they significant, and how might they be reflected in Jesus Christ's own life?

AUGUST
THE BOOK OF PROVERBS

Proverbs is a rich book. It distills much of the everyday wisdom of the ancient Israelites, and it offers us valuable counsel and advice on an array of topics. As you read Proverbs this month, look for topics that reappear throughout the book, such themes as the relation of parents and children, fidelity between husbands and wives, and the value of true friends. Notice, too, the observations made about the benefit of humility and hard work, as well as the dangers of the tongue, anger, and idleness.

In our culture, we tend to extol the virtues of "the good life." The counterpart in Israel would have been "the wise life." That's why Proverbs emphasizes so powerfully and consistently the need to attain wisdom: "Happy are those who find wisdom," we are told, because it is more precious than gold, silver, or jewels (3:13ff.).

While we view the good life as predominantly determined by material blessings (health, wealth, and happiness), Proverbs envisions the ideal life primarily in terms of moral uprightness. This kind of righteous, virtuous life would undoubtedly issue in a cascade of material blessings as well, but such blessings are only a spin-off from, not the essence of, the ideal life.

In fact, you may notice that Proverbs presents a rather bright, cheery vision of life. It does not really deal with the disturbing complexities and complications that often compel people to ask, "Why do bad things happen to good people?" Proverbs does not ask that question. It is content to delineate broad generalizations and to point out sweeping truths about life and how it ought to be lived. Proverbs accomplishes this by presenting life as two roads or paths, each with opposite directions and goals. This has been called the "two ways" doctrine, and it is the characteristic manner of thought in the Near East in ancient times, and today as well.

In Deuteronomy, for example, we read that God requires the people of Israel to choose whether they will or will not obey the Lord. They are selecting the ways either of blessing or curse, life or death (11:26; 30:15). The Sermon on the Mount in Matthew 5—7 also conveys this doctrine. "Two ways" thought underlies the Beatitudes, for instance, and it is explicit when Jesus talks about the wide and narrow gates (7:13f.) or the wise man and the foolish man (7:24ff.).

Here in Proverbs, you can glance at 4:10–19 for a particularly clear statement of the ways of wisdom and of folly. Note the stark contrast in terms of opposites: righteousness and wickedness; light and dark; peace and violence. Those who follow the way of wisdom can receive instruction, while the others are unteachable. The wise are able to follow the straight path, while the foolish stumble. The former are on the path to life; the latter are destined for death.

Basically, the whole of Proverbs was written to tell us what to do to stay on the path of wisdom. Its practical advice is aimed at keeping us from foolishly taking the wrong path, either by accident or because we are enticed by its allures and seeming pleasures. The primary way to achieve "the wise life" is to keep the commandments.

That means following God's words as they are set out in the Old Testament Scriptures.

Living after Jesus Christ has come, we can add to this—it also means following Jesus' words as they are set out in the New Testament. Isn't that exactly what Jesus said when he described the "wise man who built his house on rock" as the one who establishes his life on the words of Jesus (Matt. 7:24)?

In closing, here is a final suggestion: As you read, try underlining those verses that you find especially striking or meaningful. By the end of the month, you will probably find that the underlined verses give you a capsule summary of Proverbs. Most likely, you will also discover that you have a collection of verses that you can turn to for inspiration and encouragement in the future. Good reading!

QUESTIONS FOR REFLECTION AND DISCUSSION

PROVERBS 1

What is the origin of wisdom, according to Proverbs? Why might some people—called "fools" here—not be interested in it? How do we convince people (and ourselves) to seek after "higher things" like virtue, goodness, truth, and wisdom?

PROVERBS 3

What benefits are promised to those who seek wisdom? What does it mean in practice to "trust in the LORD"? The companion phrase is "do not rely on your own insight" (v. 5). How do you do that?

PROVERBS 6

Consider the list of six things that the Lord hates (vs. 16–19). What do each of them involve, and why are they so awful?

PROVERBS 8

Compared to many other things, wisdom is the most valuable, according to this chapter. What are some of those other things? Do any of them entice you? Wisdom is greatest, because it is pictured as participating with God in creation itself. Think about the implications of this poetic description for our understanding of God and the creation.

PROVERBS 11

A number of comparisons between the righteous and the wicked are shown here. Notice the differences in their behavior and the way their actions affect other people. How are the actions that the righteous do "wise," and how are those of the wicked "foolish"?

PROVERBS 15

Do the comments about tongues and words in the first verses of this chapter seem sensible to you? Why is it that a sharp tongue can cause so much damage, and what can we do to encourage more gracious language in our society, our homes, and our lives?

PROVERBS 19

Laziness and lack of discipline receive sharp rebukes in Proverbs. What is it about those characteristics that creates such problems for lazy or undisciplined individuals, as well as for those around them?

PROVERBS 22

You might wonder these days whether "a good name is to be chosen rather than great riches" (v. 1). Why might the writer value a good name so highly? Can you think of some people who have had good names? What are you doing that might foster or hinder your good name?

PROVERBS 25

Proverbs uses a variety of literary devices to pass on wisdom. One of them, comparisons (using "like"), occurs frequently in this chapter. Notice how vivid the images are. Pick a few—such as the comparison to a tooth and foot (v. 19)—to consider in more depth. Try to picture, or feel, the image. How does it make the comparison come alive? Which of these comparisons do you like best?

PROVERBS 28

Many of the aphorisms in Proverbs remark on how society works— especially on the level of ethical behavior, or the lack thereof.

Examine some of the observations in this chapter. Where can you find examples of similar behavior in current world and national news?

PROVERBS 31

The poem about the capable wife may be the most famous passage in the entire book. How would you describe this woman's actions and attitudes? How would you characterize her marriage to her husband? In what ways is this description applicable to contemporary life and marriage?

SEPTEMBER
THE GOSPEL OF LUKE

This month we will be reading the Gospel According to Luke. This Gospel provides a complete, well-written account of Jesus Christ's life. There's also a special warmth in this Gospel. Luke's love for his Lord comes through clearly as he writes. Let me suggest two themes to concentrate on as you read this Gospel during September.

First, *the Holy Spirit.* Luke stresses regularly the power of the Holy Spirit in Jesus' life. This is not surprising when you recall the Acts of the Apostles. There Luke placed great emphasis on the activity of the Holy Spirit in the lives of the apostles. Luke wants us to realize that God's Spirit is foundational for all of the marvelous events connected with the rise of the Christian faith.

Therefore, Luke underscores the fact that, right from the beginning of Jesus' life, God's Spirit is present and active. It is the Spirit who assures that the one born of Mary is not just a son of God, but the very incarnate Son (1:35). This same Spirit empowers Jesus, at his baptism, to conduct his earthly ministry (3:22). Watch for other references and allusions to the Spirit as you read the Gospel.

If you are wondering what all this stress on the Holy Spirit signifies for Luke, it will help to consider that Luke thinks of the Spirit, much as does the Old Testament, as "power." The Spirit is a way of referring to the incredible might of the Lord God in action in this world. Thus, by referring to the Spirit in Jesus' life, Luke means to tell us that God's Son bears the power of God in a uniquely abundant way.

But there is more to it than this. Luke also wants us to know that this same Spirit has been promised to the disciples—and indeed to all believers as well. Everyone who takes the name of Jesus Christ bears the Spirit. That is worth thinking about as we try to lead Christian lives. Too often, our attempts to live as Christians seem disturbingly weak and ineffectual. Luke would simply say: Ask the Holy Spirit to help (11:13).

Second, *a universal Gospel*. From the time of Abraham (Gen. 12:1–4), the Lord God worked through one particular people, the Jews, to furnish salvation to a needy human race. One of the primary accents of the good news of Jesus Christ is that God's mercy and grace have been extended to include all nations and peoples. That is the burden of the Great Commission at the end of Matthew 28: "Go into all the world!"

Yet not everyone was enthused by this idea. A number of Jewish Christians (like all groups who feel they are "special" in some way) were not particularly eager to share their blessings freely with others. They felt that they were superior, somehow a little better than everyone else. Thinking back to Acts again, you may recall that this was a problem even for Peter. Only because of a heavenly vision did he recognize the need to carry the gospel to the Gentiles (ch. 10).

As an "outsider" himself, Luke was especially conscious of this tendency to feel superior. That's why he points out so relent- lessly that Jesus Christ's own life bears witness to the universality of the gospel. Notice, for instance, how he sets the story of Jesus within the context of world history: Jesus is born in the reign of Augustus Caesar and enters his ministry in the time of Tiberius (2:1; 3:1). Look for cases, too, where he records that Jesus spoke about non-Israelites in the Old Testament as examples of faithful people (4:25–30; 11:29–32).

Isn't this universal emphasis worth special consideration in our day? We witness modern communications media continually shrinking our world, and we observe our economic welfare becoming increasingly tied to events and policies in other nations. Thus, to a greater degree than any generation before us, we have an opportunity to realize the import of a comment made by Paul: "There is no longer Jew or Greek, there is no longer slave or free, there is no longer male and female; for all of you are one in Christ Jesus" (Gal. 3:28). Luke would have agreed wholeheartedly!

QUESTIONS FOR REFLECTION AND DISCUSSION

LUKE 1

In Israel, childlessness was seen as a terrible tragedy, indicative of God's displeasure. Thus Elizabeth is greatly relieved to learn that she is expecting. What does her experience suggest that we should remember about God when circumstances in our own lives cause hurt, disappointment, and loss?

LUKE 2

What contrasts do you see between "Caesar" and "Christ"? What do you think Luke is trying to show us about God's relation to political powers and how God's kingdom is different from earthly kingdoms?

LUKE 5

Would you have touched the man with leprosy? What does this tell us about Jesus? Are there people around us whom only Jesus would be willing to touch? Are there ways in which you need the touch of Jesus yourself?

Luke 7

Why might John the Baptist have begun to question whether Jesus was truly the coming Messiah? How does Jesus respond, and how does that response help to clarify why Jesus came? What do Jesus' actions tell us about our own manner of living as his disciples?

Luke 9

From Jesus' sayings at the end of this chapter, it is clear that following him may not be easy. What do you think Jesus means here? Are there ways that following Jesus has been, or is, difficult for you? What have you done about it?

Luke 12

"To whom much has been given, much will be required" (v. 48) is a comment that could make us nervous. What does Jesus mean? How might the saying apply as we reflect on our own lives, our congregation, and our nation?

Luke 15

Concentrate on the older son in the parable of the prodigal son. What is he like? What is his problem? Would you want him for a friend? Notice that the father treats him with grace and compassion too. Why do you think that the parable ends without telling us whether the older brother accepts the father's invitation?

Luke 17

The story of the ten lepers cleansed by Jesus offers a sad commentary on a very human tendency. What is it? Why do you think Luke informs us that the one who returned was a Samaritan? Are there areas in your life where a prayer for healing is needed? How would you respond if your petition were granted?

Luke 19

Is the story of how you came to faith in Christ as dramatic as that of Zacchaeus? How do you know that he has been changed by meeting Jesus? Picture Jesus coming to your own house for dinner. Are there any changes you would want to make beforehand?

LUKE 23

The repentant thief on the cross is an unforgettable character found only in the Gospel of Luke. What can we learn from his story about repentance and forgiveness? What promise does Jesus make to him? How do you visualize paradise?

LUKE 24

The pilgrims on the road to Emmaus walk beside Jesus without recognizing him. How do you explain that? When does Jesus walk by our sides without being recognized? How does Jesus choose to reveal himself to the travelers, and how does he reveal himself to us?

OCTOBER
WRITINGS OF SOME MINOR PROPHETS

In October, we will be reading from those mysterious books called the "Minor Prophets." The word *prophet* means "one who speaks on behalf of another." This may serve to indicate how staggering the task of the prophet really is: The prophet is called to carry a message to Israel from the Lord God of heaven and earth! Not only that; often the prophet must enter a hostile climate to deliver this message.

There are an even dozen books of the Minor Prophets in all, too many to read profitably in one month. Thus we will focus on five of them: Hosea, Micah, Habakkuk, Joel, and Malachi. Bear in mind that each of these prophets spoke in a particular situation in Israel's history. If you are able to look for information about them in a commentary or Bible dictionary, you will be helped in understanding their messages. Here we will mention just a few overarching themes to keep in mind as you read these prophets.

First, *Israel's covenant with the Lord.* The starting point for the prophets is the covenant originally established with Abraham and developed at Mount Sinai. God freely and mercifully created a special relation with this one nation, Israel. As you can imagine, Israel took special pride in being the covenant people, for they felt that, thereby, they had been set apart as a unique nation. Unfortunately, it was easy for this justified pride in their blessings to turn into an unjustified arrogance regarding their own position and importance (Mic. 3:11).

This is where the prophets come into the picture. They point out that being special carries special responsibilities. The covenant, they remind Israel, was made with specific stipulations about how the covenant people should live. The people had received the laws of Moses, and they had agreed to keep them. Oftentimes, unfortunately, they didn't.

Second, *God's judgment on sin and disobedience.* At times, the prophets sound harsh as they excoriate the people for not living up to the commandments. Before we judge the prophets too strongly for this decidedly "unmodern" approach, it is worth recalling that the people of Israel had made solemn promises to keep the commandments. Remember, too, that the purpose of the commandments was primarily to provide for a society where mercy and help would be available for the poor—and justice and peace for all.

As you read the books of these prophets, you will notice that their descriptions convey a disturbing sense of how frequently the people have failed to exercise justice, to practice mercy, and to promote peace. In fairness to Israel, you may want to consult a newspaper to notice the similarities between their society and our own!

In the face of all of this, the message of the prophets can be put simply: There is an accounting. The unrighteous will get their just deserts. Here the mind of some of these prophets turns to the future, and their words pass over into prophecies of a final kingdom (Micah 4; Malachi 3—4). There will be a Last Day, according to Micah, when the righteous and the unrighteous will be separated. Then justice, peace, and harmony will finally reign supreme.

Third, *God's continuing mercy.* If the prophets sometimes sound harsh in their demands for righteousness, they sound positively heartwarming in their frequent reminders that God prefers mercy to judgment. The book of Hosea, with its wonderful story of Hosea's constant love for an unfaithful Gomer, provides a compelling example of the mercy of God. Hosea's willingness to take Gomer back, in spite of being hurt so badly and treated so unjustly, is a real-life parable. It directs us to a God who is ready in an instant to accept back those who have turned from the Lord.

If you are inclined to think that there is a vast difference between the God of the Old Testament and the God of the New Testament, notice how similar the story of Hosea and Gomer is to Jesus' parable about the prodigal son in Luke 15. It seems that the God we worship is more loving, more giving, and more compassionate than we can ever imagine.

If you want to reflect on a verse that can serve as a motto for all of these prophets, consider this one: "But as for me, I will look to the LORD, I will wait for the God of my salvation; my God will hear me" (Mic. 7:7).

QUESTIONS FOR REFLECTION AND DISCUSSION

HOSEA 1—3

How does Hosea's personal life portray his prophetic message of God's faithfulness? Picture the heartache that he must have experienced, as well as the fortitude he must have possessed. Have you ever had to go through a heart-wrenching experience yourself? What does this tell you about the heart of God?

HOSEA 6

The sentiment in verse 6 about God's desiring love rather than sacrifice is a regular feature of the message of the prophets. Because the Temple and ritual offerings were established as part of God's Law, how do you explain Hosea's prophecy here? What implications might this have for our own worship and religious practices?

HOSEA 9

Hosea depicts the upcoming judgment of Israel and deportation to Assyria as a punishment that will return the people to Egypt. What does Hosea mean by employing this image? How would it have been received by his hearers? What do you think would have happened if, at this point, Israel had repented?

HOSEA 11

God's compassion for Israel meets us full force in this chapter. Notice again how God's heart is broken by Israel's waywardness. In light of passages like this, how would you respond to someone who says that "the Old Testament shows us a God of wrath and judgment, while the New Testament shows us a God of grace and mercy"?

MICAH 1

The opening words of Micah announce his intention to prophesy against both Samaria (Israel) and Jerusalem (Judah). Ponder the images he uses to convey the ferocity of God's coming judgment. Does there seem to be any hope for these two kingdoms? How would you like to have been among the recipients of this message? How would you like to have been the bearer of that message?

MICAH 3

Micah decries the injustice permitted as well as practiced by the leaders in the land. What sorts of accusations does he make? How do you think the leaders would respond? What similarities or dissimilarities are there to the situation in our society?

MICAH 7

This chapter begins with "Woe is me!" and ends with praise for God's steadfast love and faithfulness. Follow Micah's thought pattern as he moves from despair to hope. Are there verses here that you need to hear in your own life?

HABAKKUK 3

After questioning God's justice sharply and sounding somewhat self-righteous in his accusations, Habakkuk affirms his own intention to remain faithful in spite of everything and anything. What kind of attitude does he portray in this chapter, and what does this suggest about how we can respond to times of trial and difficulty?

JOEL 2

This chapter prophesies amazing events that will take place at the coming of the Lord. Compare the words in verses 28 and 29 to what happens at Pentecost in Acts 2. Since prophecies about the future do not seem to be precise, line-by-line descriptions, what do you think God's purpose is in providing these portraits of the end times?

MALACHI 3—4

Malachi speaks of a messenger whom God will send to "prepare the way of the Lord." How do these chapters picture what will happen when these events occur? How do you think they relate to the appearance of John the Baptist and Jesus a few centuries later?

NOVEMBER
THE BOOK OF ISAIAH

Isaiah is a very complex book. Its sixty-six chapters (we will be reading just under half of the book this month) cover two, or perhaps three, periods in Israel's history. Not only does the book contain all-too-brief notes about the reigns of a number of kings, but it also interjects comments on social and economic life at various times. All of this makes for difficult reading!

Unless you have large blocks of time to spend in background study, the best thing to do when reading Isaiah (or the other Old Testament prophetic books, for that matter) is to concentrate on special themes in the book. Here are two themes for you to look for as you read Isaiah this month.

First, *the holiness of the Lord God.* Isaiah is struck by the awesome majesty of the Creator of heaven and earth. "Holy, holy, holy is the LORD of hosts" is the way Isaiah experiences his call to be a prophet (6:3). This awareness of God continues to undergird his message from beginning to end.

You may remember that the word *holy* means "set apart." In these early times people generally associated God (or gods) with nature. The divine was anchored inseparably in the natural realm. Thus we hear of gods of the sky and the earth, of hills and valleys, and of rivers and lakes. To suggest that God transcends nature was simply too incredible a thought for most people. Yet this is exactly what Israel's faith claimed. And this is what the book of Isaiah asserts time and time again: "I am the first and I am the last; besides me there is no god" (44:6).

Today the world looks quite different. Or does it? Are we not also tempted to trust in nature? There is the inclination to rely on our scientific, technological advances. There is the expectation that modern medicine can overcome almost any trouble or difficulty. And what of the unsettling tendency in popular movies to look to a mystical "force" in nature that will somehow provide meaning in an otherwise disturbingly cold, empty universe?

Before we become too optimistic about our technological advances or the unrealized potential for perfection in the universe, it is good to remember Isaiah's point: nature is not God, and we are not divine. We need to temper our pride in human accomplishments, lest we forget the sobering truth of the statement in the second part of the book of Isaiah: "I am the LORD" (42:6, 8).

Second, *the comforting God*. God is holy, yes, but the Lord is also compassionate. The book of Isaiah is replete with such phrases as "Comfort, O comfort my people, says your God" (40:1). To a wayward and needy people, the Lord makes thrilling promises: "For the mountains may depart and the hills be removed, but my steadfast love shall not depart from you" (54:10).

As you read, look for these kinds of phrases. Jot them down, or underline them in your Bible. Then, when you need reassurance and comfort, turn to Isaiah. You will be surprised to find how much these passages can encourage you—no matter how deep your hurt, your sorrow, or your need.

God's comfort and consolation are most striking in the picture of the suffering servant, who experiences rejection, oppression, grief, and sorrow (52:13–53:12; see 50:4–9). It is no wonder that the earliest Christians loved the book of Isaiah so much. The portrait of the suffering servant reminded them of the cross of Jesus Christ. In phrases such as "he was crushed for our iniquities" (53:5), they recognized the astounding promise that, in Christ, God offers us divine mercy, not just now, but for all eternity.

What a marvelous promise! It is designed to brace our weak knees, to rekindle hope in our despairing minds, and to pour courage into our fearful hearts. When we are touched by God's comfort, we can recognize the truth of another word in Isaiah: "Those who wait for the LORD shall renew their strength, they shall mount up with wings like eagles; they shall run and not be weary, they shall walk and not faint" (40:31).

QUESTIONS FOR REFLECTION AND DISCUSSION

ISAIAH 1

Already in this first chapter, Isaiah's words indicate God's displeasure with many things in Judah. How do the words make this clear? The words of hope in verses 16–18, however, show that the Lord offers another chance. In what areas of life might you need another chance?

ISAIAH 6

What does Isaiah's vision and call tell us about the Lord God? Do you think you would have responded as Isaiah did? What is your "call" in life?

ISAIAH 11

The traditional idea of the "sevenfold gift of the Spirit," familiar to a number of Christian denominations, is based on verse 2 of this chapter. What are the gifts mentioned here? (The seventh gift in the traditional listing, "piety," is found in the Greek translation of the Old Testament, the Septuagint.) Do you find evidence of any of

these gifts in your own life? What "spiritual gifts" would you say
you have been granted?

ISAIAH 25

This chapter points forward to a blessed future, when the earth will
be renewed. What does the prophecy say things will be like in that
day? Has there ever been a time in your life when you needed a
vision of the future to hang onto? Does this vision give you comfort?

ISAIAH 28

The words about the "foundation stone in Zion" in verse 16 are
understood in the New Testament as a prophecy of Christ (see Rom.
9:33 and 1 Pet. 2:6). What were the apostles trying to tell us by
making this connection? In what ways might you say that Jesus
Christ is your foundation stone?

ISAIAH 40

Verses 1–11 are often quoted because of their warm promises of
comfort and restoration after sorrow and desolation. How might a
despairing people hear this promise of the unexpected marvel that
Judah will return after exile in Babylon? What do these words tell
us about our God?

ISAIAH 45

The words in verse 22, "I am God, and there is no other," echo a
regular theme throughout this and the surrounding chapters. It
seems that Israel is not really convinced that God is the only God,
perhaps not even the most significant God. In light of the Exodus
and other "big events" in Israel's history, how could the people have
had what appear to be such serious doubts?

ISAIAH 55

It is hard to find a chapter that contains richer and more beautiful
imagery than this one. What is said here about God's promises,
God's mercies, and God's word? Can you describe times when some
of the things proclaimed here have been evident in your own life?

ISAIAH 56

Verse 7 depicts a general divine pledge to redeem all peoples. Why might ancient Israel have thought that they alone had been chosen by God? What other peoples and groups have thought that they were "special"? Is it easy to believe that we are somehow unique in God's eyes? What are the dangers in such a belief?

ISAIAH 61

When Jesus returns to Nazareth and preaches in the synagogue (Luke 4:16– 30), he applies the first two verses of this chapter to his own ministry. How do these words point to what Jesus is about to do?

ISAIAH 65

"New heavens and a new earth" are promised in this chapter (v. 17). How does Isaiah delineate life in this new world? How would you visualize a truly renewed world? What will it take to get to a world that is really new?

DECEMBER
THE GOSPEL OF JOHN

We have reached the final month of the "Bible Book of the Month" program! I hope that these readings have helped to increase your sense of the significance of these major books of the Bible. In this final month, we will be reading the Gospel of John. With its accent on the incarnation of the Savior, it will make for splendid reading in the Advent season.

By the time John was written, the three Synoptic Gospels were already in circulation. John does not repeat their basically chronological presentation. Rather, this Gospel aims to present a more in-depth portrait of Jesus. This feature of the Gospel so impressed one of the early Church Fathers, Origen, that he called John a "spiritual Gospel."

This phrase captures the essence of John. Above all else, the book is concerned to take us to the inner side of life. There is much more to human existence, John tells us, than the hustle and bustle we perceive around us. The world, with its unceasing physical activity, is only the surface level of events. If that is difficult to grasp, then recall the astounding claims made by modern physics: Our world may seem solid and firm, but in reality it is composed of innumerable subatomic particles—invisible building blocks that appear to be more energy than matter.

Now, of course, John is not talking about nuclear physics. He is addressing something even more amazing—the invisible connection of the world to God. The book does this by regularly pointing to two levels of reality. Various things in our physical realm hint at a deeper, more profound reality. As you read this month, look for places where the Gospel implies two levels. To help you along, here are two features of the book that constantly direct us to a deeper level of meaning.

First, *the seven signs.* As you read the first eleven chapters of John, be on the lookout for seven extraordinary actions that Jesus performs. Each sign carries a profound message about Jesus that goes beyond the deed itself.

A glance at the final sign, the raising of Lazarus from the dead in chapter 11, illustrates this. In performing this marvel, Jesus illustrates the fact that he has power over death and the grave. The sign, therefore, provides a foretaste of his own resurrection, but it also proclaims a thrilling message about our future as well. Contrary to the surface appearance of things, at our death we are not condemned to cease existing; rather, in Christ we have the sure promise that our lives will continue for all eternity. Like this seventh sign, the preceding six signs offer us an array of insights into who Jesus is and what he does. As you locate the six, pause to consider the deeper meaning of each of them.

Second, *the "I am's."* Just as there are seven signs, there are seven statements made by Jesus that begin, "I am." One of these declarations occurs in the story of Lazarus mentioned above, when Jesus affirms, "I am the resurrection and the life" (11:25). Can you find the other six statements?

In each of these declarations, Jesus' statement pushes us to think more deeply. First, it prompts us to realize that spiritual realities have greater significance than the tangible, earthly things around us. Second, it encourages us to recognize that we touch these spiritual realities decisively when we are attached to Jesus Christ himself.

One further thing about the "I am's." They are a deliberate allusion to the name of God given to Moses at the burning bush: "I AM WHO I AM" (Ex. 3:14). In other words, these statements point us to the fact that Jesus Christ is not simply the one who brings God's salvation into the world. This Jesus, who comes to us as a babe at Christmas, is also God.

That was an incredible thought back then. It still is. Yet, as John intends to make crystal clear, our hope and our salvation hang on this truth: "But these are written so that you may come to believe that Jesus is the Messiah, the Son of God, and that through believing you may have life in his name" (20:31).

QUESTIONS FOR REFLECTION AND DISCUSSION

JOHN 1

What does it mean to call Jesus the "Word" of God? How does this tie together with his bringing light into the world? Who is Jesus Christ for you, and what kind of impact does he have on your life?

JOHN 3

Jesus' discussion with Nicodemus touches on some major points about the Gospel: the new birth, faith, grace, the cross, and the Spirit. Why are these concepts so hard for Nicodemus to grasp? Do they make sense to you? Which one is most difficult? Which gives you special comfort?

JOHN 5

Look at the events in this chapter through the eyes of the paralytic at Bethzatha. How would he have felt at the beginning of the story, as Jesus is talking to him, and then afterward, when he has been healed? Why might the Jews be so upset about a healing on the

Sabbath? Does your congregation—or do you yourself—have any rules (possibly unwritten or unspoken) that may get in the way of relationships with other people?

JOHN 6

What does Jesus mean by saying that we need to eat his flesh and drink his blood? How does this relate to faith and eternal life? Do you think there is any connection to the Lord's Supper here? If so, how would you describe that connection?

JOHN 9

After all that has been said in this Gospel about light, why is it significant that Jesus heals a blind man in this chapter? What do you think of the reaction of this man's parents? Name a time in your life when you have been "blind" and have needed Christ's healing touch.

JOHN 11

Drawing on this chapter, along with Luke 10:38–41, how would you describe Mary, Martha, and Lazarus and their relationship to Jesus? By raising Lazarus, Jesus tells us who he is, as well as what he is doing in bringing resurrection and eternal life. What does this passage say about Christ and about resurrection from the dead?

JOHN 13

The foot washing teaches us not only that Jesus, the Lord, acts as a servant, but also that we are to be servants in turn. In a culture such as ours—marked by individualism, independence, and self-sufficiency—what kind of response would you expect to Jesus' action? In what ways can you take a towel to serve in your family, your community, your church?

JOHN 14

Why do the disciples need comfort, and what kind of consolation does Jesus promise here? How will the Spirit, the Advocate, be of use? What does it mean to say that the Spirit will "abide" in us, and what are the implications of that reality for our daily living?

JOHN 17

This chapter is sometimes called the "high priestly prayer of Jesus." Take a close look at what Jesus prays for here. What main themes can you find, and what do you learn about Jesus himself from this prayer? Think about your own prayers. What do they tell you about yourself? How can Jesus' prayer serve as a model for us in growing in our prayer life?

JOHN 18

Simon Peter is a study in contrasts in this chapter. How can he go from one characteristic to the opposite so quickly? Are you usually more like Peter in the garden, or Peter by the fire? In either case, what do you need from Christ to enable you more and more to be a faithful disciple?

JOHN 21

Simon Peter is also at the center of this chapter. Notice how he takes the lead in the action in the first half of the chapter. Notice, too, how much space the Gospel gives to the conversation between Jesus and Peter. What is the significance of Jesus' final instructions to Peter? What meaning might the words about feeding sheep have to today's disciples?